Foundations – Faith Life Essentials
Transmitting God's Power

© 2007 Derek Prince Ministries–International
This edition DPM-UK 2020
ISBN 978-1-78263-551-2
Product Code: B106D

This message is a transcript book with questions and study suggestions added by the Derek Prince Ministries editorial team.

DPM
Derek Prince Ministries
www.derekprince.com

EXPANDED
VERSION:
GROUP
STUDY

Transmitting
God's Power

DPM

DEREK PRINCE MINISTRIES - UK

Contents

About This Study Series

The Bible is God's Word and our "instruction manual" to find the path to salvation in Jesus. It then shows us how to walk with Him once we have come to know Him. Logically, therefore, it is a hugely important part of our challenge as Christian believers to study the Word of God.

A sad fact is that very often we forget most of what we have heard quite quickly! As a result, what we have heard often has little impact on the way that we continue to live.

That is why we developed these Study Guides. As Derek Prince has said numerous times in his teaching, "It is a general principle of educational psychology that children remember approximately 40 percent of what they hear; 60 percent of what they hear and see and 80 percent of what they hear, see and do."

This Study Guide is intended to help you to assimilate the truths that you have heard into both your head and into your heart so that they become more than just knowledge and will begin to change the way that you live.

Living the Christian life

This study is part of a series of 10 messages, based on the doctrinal foundation of the Christian Life described in Hebrews 6:1-2 which says,

> *Therefore, leaving the discussion of the elementary principles of Christ, let us go on to perfection, not laying again the foundation of repentance from dead works and of faith*

toward God, of the doctrine of baptisms, of laying on of hands, of resurrection of the dead, and of eternal judgment.

This mentions six specific foundation stones that we need to lay before we can build a dwelling place for the Lord in our hearts and lives:

1. Repentance from dead works
2. Faith towards God
3. The doctrine of baptisms – John's baptism, Christian baptism and baptism in the Holy Spirit
4. Laying on of hands
5. Resurrection of the dead
6. Eternal judgment.

When this teaching is applied in your life, with faith, we believe that it will deepen your relationship with God and enable you to live a truly successful Christian life.

How to Study

Each book contains a QR-code (or DVD) that links you to a talk by Derek Prince, the transcript of the talk and questions for personal application or to be discussed in a group setting.

Each video is about an hour long, divided in three parts. Set aside a reasonable length of time to read the Introduction, then watch or read Derek's teaching, and finally come back to the Study Guide to reflect on the Study Questions or to discuss them with your study group.

Once you have completed this series you will find that you have an excellent summary of the teaching. This will help you to share the content with others, whether to a friend, home group or congregation. The more you share the truths you are learning, the more they will become part of your own life and testimony.

Group Study

This study guide has been developed for use by small groups as well as by individuals.

Simply proceed through the material as a team, reflect on the questions and explore the statements together for a rich and rewarding experience.

Scripture to Memorize

In this book, we have chosen key Scriptures for memorization. They will relate in some way to your overall study. Memorizing them will place a spiritual sword in your hands which you, by the Holy Spirit, will be able to use in times of spiritual conflict.

The Word of God has supernatural power for those who will take the time and effort to "hide it in their hearts" by memorizing and meditating on it. As God's Word is hidden in your heart, it becomes constantly available to you for reference, comfort, correction and meditation. Put simply, it becomes part of your life.

Look up the verse in your own Bible and write it in the space provided. You will want to write and say this verse out loud several times until you are confident you know it well. Take time to meditate on the words and their application to your life. As a group, you could talk briefly about the meaning of the verse and its relevance to the lesson or share how you applied it.

You will be asked to recall your Memory Work at the end of the book.

Transmitting God's Power – an Introduction

In this study, you are going to learn about the **Laying on of Hands** which, despite being a foundational doctrine, is seldom taught about. You may be surprised to find it listed in Hebrews 6 but it is extremely logical as an essential part of the Christian life.

This ordinance gives continuity between a senior minister and a junior minister and between one generation and the next. You will look at examples from the Old Testament of laying on of hands as a means to impart blessing, determine destiny, set apart, endorse, equip and to impart supernatural spiritual authority.

Then, Derek Prince will go on to teach from the New Testament on the many purposes for the laying on of hands in the age of the Church before noting some dangers you need to be aware of and providing helpful safeguards.

In all his teaching, Derek Prince not only sought to impart knowledge, but revelation of the Word through the Spirit with the ultimate goal of love. May that be your experience as you start your study on *Transmitting God's Power*.

Watch Derek Prince's teaching *Transmitting God's Power* on YouTube. Scan the QR-code or visit dpmuk.org/foundations.

This video has been divided into three sections, following the chapters in this book. You will find the links to these sections when you tap the 'down arrow' to expand the information about the video.

Write down these verses and try to memorize them.

James 5:14

----

1 Timothy 5:22

Laying on of hands is an essential element in the history of God's people.

Transmitting God's Power

This is the fourth of the foundation doctrines listed in Hebrews 6:1–2, the laying on of hands, which I have rendered "Transmitting God's Power."

Many of us would probably be a little surprised to find that laying on of hands is among the foundation doctrines, because very little is said about it currently in most congregations. If we pause and consider, it is extremely logical that it is there—because laying on of hands (or transmitting God's power and authority) is that which brings continuity to the body of Christ. Continuity is established between a senior minister and a junior minister and between one generation and the next. The essential function of this ministry of laying on of hands is to provide continuity in the body of Christ.

Some traditions claim to have preserved this continuity from the days of the apostle Peter until now. I am not considering that claim, but I will point out that the reasoning behind it is logical. We need a way to continue from generation to generation, from ministry to ministry. The way has been provided in the Scripture by this ordinance of laying on of hands.

We find the laying on of hands in the first book of the Bible and we can see it extends from then on through the whole history of God's people. It is an essential element in the history of God's people.

There are certain spiritual purposes it embraces. First, let's recognize the fact that to put your hand on somebody is a natural, human reaction. A mother who has a sick baby with a fever, almost without reasoning will put her hand on the forehead of the child. Or, two men may meet who have not seen one another for awhile and in one way or another they will make contact with their hands—they will lay their hands on each other's shoulders or shake hands. We see that the hand is one of the main ways for human beings to make contact with one another.

To Transmit

In the spiritual context, I suggest that there are certain purposes that are accomplished. First of all, in the Bible we find the laying on of hands is used to transmit blessings, authority, wisdom, the Holy Spirit, a spiritual gift, or a ministry.

To Commission

Second, it is the biblical way to commission a person for a place of service in the body of Christ.

As such, first of all, it recognizes God's appointment. We need to understand that appointments in the Church are not settled by voting. God is not subject to votes. A lot of churches vote for deacons or pastors or for some other function, but that really is not scriptural. It is God who makes the appointments. Jesus said to His apostles, "You did not choose Me, but I chose you" (John 15:16). That is true of every valid function, ministry and appointment in the Church. It is not man who made the choice, but God—because Jesus Christ is head over all things to the Church which is His body. Appointments that are not made on the authority of Jesus really have no validity. But the appointment is not to make a person a certain thing, but to recognize what God has decided that person should be. If there is a meeting in church to discuss the appointment of deacons, our purpose should not be to decide who we would like to have as a deacon. Our purpose should be to decide whom God has chosen as a deacon. It is a very different attitude. We are somewhat corrupted by democracy, which has very little place in the Bible or in the Church. This is a rather controversial issue.

Second, apart from recognizing God's choice, laying on of hands is used to set apart for a certain task or ministry.

Third, it is used to endorse or to give authority.

Fourth, it is used to equip; that is, to transmit the spiritual gift or authority needed to carry out God's appointed task.

To recap, the function of laying on of hands in commissioning people is used to recognize, but not appoint, the persons of God's choice. It is used to set apart a person to a certain task or ministry. It is used to endorse a person with authority. And it is used to equip a person with all the spiritual authority or gifts that person will need.

Examples from the Old Testament

First of all, we will turn to Genesis 48, which is a very interesting passage. Joseph has brought his two sons to his father Jacob (who is also called Israel) for him to bless his grandsons. Let me say that, second to the blessing of God Himself, the most desired blessing is one given by a father or grandfather. I would say to everyone, especially younger people, if by any means possible, that you obtain your father's blessing on whatever you do. In the Bible, great importance was attached to a father's blessing.

> Then Israel [or Jacob] *saw Joseph's sons, and said, "Who are these?" And Joseph said to his father, "They are my sons, whom God has given me in this place* [Egypt]*." And he* [Jacob]

said, "Please bring them to me, and I will bless them." Now
the eyes of Israel were dim with age, so that he could not see.
Then Joseph brought them near him, and he kissed them
and embraced them. And Israel said to Joseph, "I had not
thought to see your face; but in fact, God has also shown me
your offspring!"
Genesis 48:8–11

If there is one thing that moves me to tears, it is the faithfulness of God. Every time I contemplate the faithfulness of God, I am overcome with tears.

So Joseph brought them from beside his knees, and he bowed
down with his face to the earth. [Notice the respect that
people in the Bible showed for parents and for the elderly.]
And Joseph took them both, Ephraim with his right hand
toward Israel's left hand, and Manasseh with his left hand
toward Israel's right hand, and brought them near him. Then
Israel stretched out his right hand and laid it on Ephraim's
head, who was the younger, and his left hand on Manasseh's
head, guiding his hands knowingly, for Manasseh was the
firstborn. verses 13–14

Normally, the firstborn would receive the greater blessing, which would be transmitted by the right hand. Joseph specially arranged that Manasseh, who was the elder, was to come opposite Jacob's right hand. But Jacob, prompted by the Holy Spirit, crossed his hands and laid his right hand on Ephraim and his left hand on Manasseh.

He blessed Joseph, and said: "God, before whom my fathers
Abraham and Isaac walked, the God who has fed me all my
life long to this day, the angel who has redeemed me from
all evil [this happened when Jacob met the angel at Peniel
in Genesis 32:22–32.] *Bless the lads; let my name be named*
upon them, and the name of my fathers Abraham and Isaac;

and let them grow into a multitude in the midst of the earth."
verses 15–16

We can see how important it is to transmit a name. So many biblical practices are going out of fashion today, but they have never gone out of fashion with God.

Now when Joseph saw that his father laid his right hand on the head of Ephraim, it displeased him; so he took hold of his father's hand to remove it from Ephraim's head to Manasseh's head. And Joseph said to his father, "Not so, my father, for this one is the firstborn; put your right hand on his head." But his father refused and said, "I know, my son, I know. He also shall become a people, and he also shall be great; but truly his younger brother shall be greater than he, and his descendants shall become a multitude of nations." So he blessed them that day, saying, "By you Israel will bless, saying, 'May God make you as Ephraim and as Manasseh!'" And thus he set Ephraim before Manasseh. verses 17–20

That is a very vivid scene and it is very precise. It was understood that the greater blessing would come from the father's right hand. And it was so real that there was a real transmission of blessing; it was not just a formality or ceremony. It was a vital transaction in the lives of two young men, Ephraim and Manasseh. It determined their destiny from then onward.

Let us never underestimate the significance and the importance of laying on of hands when it is done by the Holy Spirit.

The next example is in Numbers 27, where we find that Moses was telling the Lord that it was time to appoint the leader who was to follow him. Moses knew that he would not enter the Promised Land, but he was very concerned about Israel, the people of God. So Moses said to the Lord:

Then Moses spoke to the Lord, saying: "Let the Lord, the God of the spirits of all flesh, set a man over the congregation."
Numbers 27:15

It is significant that God is "the God of the spirits of all flesh"—He knows the spirit of every person. He sees into the innermost depth of human character.

"Let the Lord, the God of the spirits of all flesh, set a man over the congregation, who may go out before them and go in before them, who may lead them out and bring them in, that the congregation of the Lord may not be like sheep which have no shepherd." verses 16–17

The whole Bible tells us from beginning to end that sheep without a shepherd will be scattered and will become a prey. It is a message that runs consistently throughout the Bible. Let me suggest that unless circumstances are very unusual, each person should have a human shepherd who will watch over your soul and care for you—it is very important.

How did the Lord respond?

The Lord said to Moses: "Take Joshua the son of Nun with you, a man in whom is the Spirit, and lay your hand on him; set him before Eleazar the priest and before all the congregation, and inaugurate [commission] him in their sight. And you shall give some of your authority to him." verses 18–20

I like that: not "all of your authority," because Moses had unique authority. But, give him a good portion of your authority, because he is going to need it.

"You shall give some of your authority to him, that all the congregation of the children of Israel may be obedient.

He shall stand before Eleazar the priest, who shall inquire
  before the Lord for him by the judgment of the Urim. At his
  word [Joshua's word] they shall go out, and at his word they
  shall come in, he and all the children of Israel with him—all
  the congregation." So Moses did as the Lord commanded
  him. He took Joshua and set him before Eleazar the priest
  and before all the congregation. And he laid his hands on
  him and inaugurated [commissioned] him, just as the Lord
  had commanded by the hand of Moses. verses 20–23

You see, the whole congregation had to witness this transmission of authority from Moses—the one whom they followed for forty years—to his successor. It was a vital transaction for the well being of all of God's people.

Furthermore, it was not just a ceremony, something really happened to Joshua. In Deuteronomy 34, we have this interesting comment.

Now Joshua the son of Nun was full of the spirit of wisdom,
  for Moses had laid his hands on him.
  Deuteronomy 34:9

We see that through the laying on of hands Joshua received the spirit of wisdom. It was not just a formality or ceremony. It was a genuine transaction.

For our last Old Testament example, we will go to 2 Kings 13, which is the closing scene in the life of Elisha.

Elisha had become sick of the illness of which he would die.
  2 Kings 13:14

This is certainly not what one would expect. He died of a sickness, yet his bones were so charged with the power of God that when a dead man contacted his bones, the dead man came alive (see verses 20–21). We cannot explain that. There are some things that are beyond explanation.

Let me relate something that happened to me, because people are always trying to account for everything that God does. In South Africa some years ago Ruth and I were ministering in an Assembly of God Church. The associate pastor, who was a young man, had been playing squash, and he had fallen and broken his arm in four places. So he came to us for prayer. I said, "I know this sounds strange, but I'm going to check your legs because this is what God has shown me to do. If your legs are unequal, the short leg will grow out and you will know that God has touched you." Then I said, "Be very careful to thank God for it." You see, when people have a real need, they will do all sorts of strange things they would never do at other times.

So he went through this ceremony: I held his legs and one of them grew out. I knew God had touched him. He went back to the doctor and was X-rayed. This is what I cannot explain: there had been four breaks in his arm. Three of them were perfectly healed, the fourth was still broken. The senior pastor said to me, "Explain that!" I can't explain it. I could say, "He had seventy-five percent faith," but that would be a very unconvincing explanation. People think they know everything God has done and are able to explain it all. But there are lots of things God does that I cannot explain. I am quite content to leave them with God.

As we go on with this story:

> Then Joash the king of Israel came down to [Elisha], and wept over his face, and said, "O my father, my father, the chariots of Israel and their horsemen!" verses 14–15

That was the same thing Elisha had said to Elijah when he was taken up in the chariot (see 2 Kings 2:11). And it contains a message for all of us, really. A man who really knows God can be the defense of a nation, he can be stronger than an army. Joash, who was not a particularly godly king, recognized what Elisha meant to his people.

> *And Elisha said to him, "Take a bow and some arrows." So he took himself a bow and some arrows. Then he said to the king of Israel, "Put your hand on the bow." So he [the king] put his hand on it [the bow] and Elisha put his hands on the king's hands. And he said, "Open the east window" [which was the direction of Syria, the enemy of Israel]; and he opened it. Then Elisha said, "Shoot"; and he shot. And he said, "The arrow of the Lord's deliverance and the arrow of deliverance from Syria; for you must strike the Syrians at Aphek till you have destroyed them." verses 15–17*

We read that Joash struck with the arrows three times and we find out that three times Joash defeated the Syrians. Elisha was angry with him because he should have struck more times. What I want to bring out here is that what made it effective was Elisha's putting his hands on the hands of the king when he held the bow. Again, it is in the supernatural realm, but it shows that a real impartation can take place when one person lays hands on another.

Study Questions

Group study / personal reflection

1. What special insights did you gain from this lesson?

   ----

2. Laying on of hands is not a common practice in most churches. On what occasions have you witnessed it being done? By whom, and for what purpose?

   ----

3. Why does laying on of hands need to be part of the foundational doctrines of the Christian Church (see Hebrew 6:1-2)?

---

4. Laying on of hands is an essential element in the history of God's people. Read the verses below. For what purpose were hands laid on, and by whom?

- Genesis 48:8-15 _____

- Leviticus 1:1-4 _____

- Leviticus 8:5-22 _____

- Numbers 27:17-24 _____

- Matthew 19:13-15 _____

- Luke 4:40 _____

- Acts 8:15-19 _____

- 1 Timothy 4:13-14 _____

- Acts13:1-3_____

5. In order to appoint pastors or deacons we need to recognize what God has decided a person should be. How could you recognize that?

----

6. Derek Prince lists four purposes for the laying on of hands. Can you give examples of each of them from the Church today?

  • ---

  • ---

  • ---

  • ---

7. Second to the blessing of God Himself, the most desired blessing is one given by a parent or grandparent. If you are a parent or grandparent yourself, consider blessing your child this week by laying on of hands. How would you want them to be blessed? Have you ever been blessed by an authority figure?

----

8. Read the story in Genesis 48 and consider how Joseph blessed his grandchildren. What stands out for you in his words?

----

9. Is blessing a person different to praying for them? If so, in what way?

----

10. Read Genesis 48:15-16, Numbers 27:15-23, Deuteronomy 34:9 and 2 Kings 13:15-17. A blessing is not just a ceremony but a real transmission. What did Jacob (Israel), Moses and Elisha transmit?

SUMMARY

- Laying on of hands is a real transaction – it is not just a formality or just for ceremony. It can determine someone's destiny.

- In the Bible we find the laying on of hands used to transmit blessings, authority, wisdom, the Holy Spirit, a spiritual gift or a ministry. It is the biblical way of commissioning a person for a place of service in the body of Christ and as such, it recognizes God's appointment.

- In commissioning, there are four key functions of laying on of hands:
    - To recognize - not to appoint, but rather recognize God's choice.
    - To set apart - to a given task or ministry.
    - To endorse – to place an authoritative seal on the person being commissioned.
    - To equip - by transmitting spiritual authority.

The laying on of hands is not limited merely to people with a special ministry.

Purposes Indicated in the New Testament

Let's now consider the purposes indicated in the New Testament for the laying on of hands.

To impart healing

First of all, to impart healing to the sick. Jesus said when He commissioned His disciples to God, "These signs shall follow those who believe" (Mark 16:17). The fifth sign was, "They will lay hands on the sick, and they will recover" (verse 18). In other words, laying hands on the sick was a way of ministering God's healing to them.

In James 5:14–15 we find another ordinance:

Is anyone among you sick? Let him call for the elders of the church, and let them pray over him, anointing him with oil in the name of the Lord. And the prayer of faith will save the sick, and the Lord will raise him up.

The elders are to pray over him. They are to lay hands on him, but they are also to anoint him with oil. As I am sure we know, oil is always a type of the Holy Spirit. The oil does not produce the healing, but it symbolizes the release of the Holy Spirit through that ceremony into the body of the sick person.

What is the difference between just laying on hands or laying on hands and anointing with oil? I suggest to you, and this is just approximate—that the laying on of hands without the anointing of oil was for people who were not members of the church. But for members of the church, the ordinance included anointing with oil.

Again, I want to point out that the New Testament indicates that normally every believer should be part of a congregation, for he says, "Is anyone [Christians] among you sick? Let him call for the elders of the church, and let them pray over him, anointing him with oil." If we go to one church on Sunday morning and another church on Sunday evening, which group of elders will we call for? And if we do not have elders to call for, what will we do when we are sick? In other words, the New Testament assumes, with various exceptions, that a believer shall be a member of a congregation. He should be known to the leadership, recognize their leadership, and have available to him the ministry of the leadership.

Just let me back that up with another Scripture. This is not on this particular subject, but in the book of Revelation, chapters 2 and 3, there are seven messages sent to seven churches—but only to the churches. Anybody who was not in a church did not get the message. I feel God wants me to emphasize this point. Some people are like mountain goats—they are way out ahead of the herd and don't have a shepherd. That is a dangerous place to be. It is humbling to submit yourself to human authority, but God blesses the humble and He resists the proud (1 Peter 5:5). We have to choose.

There are exceptions and situations where this does not apply. But we should not be an exception if we should be part of the rule.

To impart the Holy Spirit

In Acts 8 we read about Philip, who went to a city of Samaria and preached Christ, attested by miracles and signs, and all the people in the city who believed were baptized. They were saved because Jesus said, "He who believes and is baptized will be saved" (Mark

16:16). But the apostles were not content because they knew there was something missing.

> Now when the apostles who were at Jerusalem heard that Samaria had received the word of God, they sent Peter and John to them, who, when they had come down, prayed for them that they might receive the Holy Spirit. For as yet He had fallen upon none of them. They had only been baptized in the name of the Lord Jesus.
> Acts 8:14–16

That is a very clear indication that it is possible to be saved without having received the Holy Spirit. The Holy Spirit spoken of there as "falling upon them," is what I call immersion from above—a Niagara Falls immersion.

> Then they [the apostles] *laid hands on them, and they* [the believers] *received the Holy Spirit. And when Simon* [the magician] *saw that through the laying on of the apostles' hands the Holy Spirit was given, he offered them money, saying, "Give me this power also." verses 17–19*

In the next chapter, after Saul had his encounter with Jesus on the Damascus road, while he was there in a house in Damascus, unable to see, and fasting for three days, Ananias, a mere disciple—not an apostle or prophet, just a disciple—came to him. He had received directions from the Lord to go to the house where Saul was, lay hands on him and pray for him. When Ananias laid hands on Saul, his sight was restored and he was baptized in the Holy Spirit. We need to understand, the laying on of hands is not limited merely to people with a special ministry. In the context of God's will, any person can be directed to lay hands on someone else.

I have a rather unusual story to relate concerning this. Ruth and I were in Kona, Hawaii, and I had been very sick. In fact, I was still far from recovered. We were walking down the main street and a man came up to us and said, "Will you pray for me? I'm sick." I said, "What's the matter with you?" He said, he had been electrocuted, he had received a full charge (he was an electrician).

His shoulders were paralyzed and he could not raise his arms. I was rather reluctant to do it, in a way, but he was persistent. So we stopped in the middle of the street right outside a restaurant and we prayed. Ruth laid her hands on his shoulders. The next day in the devotions at Youth With A Mission he put his hands right up above his head. He had experienced a miracle through the laying on of hands!

Later on he came to see us, when we were ministering in Arizona, and told us that he had been to a doctor for a check up. The doctor said, "I've examined your shoulders. There is no possible way that you could ever get your arms above your head!" Well, that is an example of what the laying on of hands will do.

In Acts 19 we read that Paul arrived in Ephesus and found there certain disciples of the teachings of John the Baptist as taught by Apollos. Paul explained the gospel to them, they were baptized in the name of the Lord Jesus, and, when Paul laid his hands on them, they spoke with tongues and prophesied. (See Acts 19:1–6.) So we see that laying on of hands is a very scriptural way to transmit the power of the Holy Spirit.

Actually, there are five main examples of receiving the baptism in the Holy Spirit in the New Testament. In two cases—on the Day of Pentecost (Acts 2:1–4) and in the house of Cornelius (Acts 10:44–48)—it came sovereignly from God. In the other three cases—in Samaria (Acts 8:14–20), with Saul of Tarsus (Acts 9:17–18) and in Ephesus (Acts 19:1–6)—it was transmitted through the laying on of hands. It is a question of how God leads.

I have had the privilege of leading literally thousands of people into the baptism in the Holy Spirit. My particular strength is to get people to believe that if they seek the Lord, they will receive. I do lay hands on people. However, I can say, by the grace of God, I have seen thousands of people receive direct from the Lord.

To commission church servants

The next purpose of laying on of hands is to commission servants of the church, sometimes called deacons. I wonder how some churches would change if they realized that the word deacon in Greek means "a servant." In some churches the Board of Deacons has a lot of authority. How would it be if they were called the Board of Servants? We have gotten some of our terminology mixed up.

It was taken for granted in the New Testament Church that they invariably accepted responsibility for their widows. In Acts 6, the Church had run into a very good problem—they were growing so fast that they could not take care of all the poor and the widows who needed their attention. The problem today is that the government has taken over so many functions that the Church does not really realize its responsibilities. I believe the Church has a responsibility for the poor, whatever way that responsibility may be carried out.

The believers came to the apostles and said, "Things aren't working out right, our widows are being neglected." So the apostles said they would take steps. This was a rather crucial situation. The twelve apostles summoned the congregation and said:

> "It is not desirable that we should leave the word of God and serve tables. Therefore, brethren, seek out from among you seven men of good reputation, full of the Holy Spirit and wisdom, whom we may appoint over this business; but we will give ourselves continually to prayer and to the ministry of the word."
> Acts 6:2–4

The apostolic ministry is prayer and the ministry of the Word, not administration. They said they could get other people to do the administration, but they needed to stick with their responsibility. So they said, "Choose seven men from among you whom you know." All of them had to be full of the Holy Spirit. Not even a deacon was appointed in the early Church unless he was full of the Holy Spirit.

This was the wisdom of the apostles, you see. The apostles were going to look after the finances, but they let the congregation choose the men. The apostles accepted the men, ordained them and put them in office. After that, the congregation could never complain about the men because the congregation made the choice. See how wise God is?

So it says the congregation brought these men and "set [them] before the apostles; and when they had prayed, they laid hands on them" (verse 6). They were ordaining them. The apostles were getting so busy they needed helpers.

The position of a helper was very important. It is interesting to see what happened to two of those helpers: Stephen became the first martyr and Philip became the God-acknowledged evangelist. Brother or sister, if you start in the position of a servant, bear in mind it can be a steppingstone to something else. In fact, if you don't start as a servant, you really never will be promoted by God because God only promotes people who start down the ladder.

To send out apostles

The next purpose of the laying on of hands is to send out apostles. Some people think there are only twelve apostles in the New Testament. That is not so. I have counted approximately twenty people who were called apostles. There were the twelve foundation apostles, then there were other apostles who were mentioned by name. We will look at some of them.

In Acts 13 it speaks about the church at Antioch, which was in many ways a model church. In fact, in some ways it got ahead of the church in Jerusalem, which got a little bit stuck in what I would call "internal focus." That is one of the big problems with our churches today. Most churches are so focused on the internal that they have very little time for the real job, which is preaching the gospel to those who have never heard it. But the people at Antioch had a different vision and this is very important.

> Now in the church that was at Antioch there were certain prophets and teachers [five of them are named]: Barnabas, Simeon, Lucius, Manaen and Saul [who later became Paul]. Acts 13:1

If we can believe for prophets and teachers, then the way is open for apostles.

> As they ministered to the Lord [worshiped the Lord, NIV] and fasted, the Holy Spirit said, "Now separate to Me Barnabas and Saul for the work to which I have called them." verse 2

Notice, the Holy Spirit was speaking as God: "Separate to Me these two men." How do you think the Holy Spirit said it? Do you think it was a disembodied voice that came, or do you think He spoke through one of the five men? You can make up your own mind—I believe personally it was probably a prophetic word.

> Then, having fasted and prayed, and laid hands on them, they sent them away. verse 3

I am a great believer in fasting and prayer. A lot of happenings in the church will never occur until people learn to fast and pray. This was the second time they had fasted. They were already fasting when they got the message.

Please note, they did not just choose the junior youth director, which is what some churches would do. They chose the two top men; they sent out their best. Promotion to the outreach of the ministry is from the top, not from the bottom. The Church of today has a tremendous lesson to learn. The people who are "missionaries" (or whatever you want to call them) are not people with some minor ministry way on down the line; they should be the top people chosen by God. We have an altogether wrong emphasis on our internal structure and we are so absorbed with ourselves that we really do not have the vision of the Lord.

I hope you will forgive me for saying this, but many people in the current move of the Holy Spirit, at least in some countries, are like the astronomers in the days of Ptolemy. I do not know much about astronomy, but Ptolemy was convinced that the sun revolved around the earth. Along came Copernicus and he said, "That's not right; it's the other way around. The earth revolves around the sun." Typically enough, the Church wanted to put Copernicus to death for saying that. He just escaped with his life.

Why was the Church so upset? Because Copernicus' theory was contrary to their traditions.

I say, a lot of Christians are still living in the age of Ptolemy. They still believe that God the Son revolves around us. They have not yet learned it is the other way around. We revolve around the Son. Jesus is not here for our benefit; we are here for His glory. Some of the songs we sing focus entirely on what Jesus will do for us. That's wonderful, but the emphasis should be on what we will do for Jesus.

The church at Antioch sent out its two best men. When they were sent out they were prophets and teachers, but if you read on in the next chapter of Acts about the same two men, it says at one point:

The multitude of the city was divided: part sided with the Jews, and part with the apostles. . . . But when the apostles

Barnabas and Paul heard this . . .
Acts 14:4, 14

We see that Barnabas and Paul had become apostles. How had they become apostles? By being sent out from a church through the direction of the Holy Spirit.

The meaning of the word apostle is "one who is sent out." If we have not been sent out we are not an apostle. Here are two men who were not in the original twelve, who are now called apostles. They become apostles by the appointment of the Holy Spirit. They heard the voice of the Holy Spirit when they were praying, fasting and worshiping God. When church leadership follows that sequence, then we will see apostles emerging.

MY NOTES

Study Questions

1. In this study, was there anything specific that was new or stood out for you?

    ....

    ....

    ....

    ....

2. In the Bible, the laying on of hands always had a definite spiritual purpose. Which one?

    ....

    ....

    ....

    ....

3. Discuss/reflect: Laying hands on the sick for healing should be practised by all Jesus' followers. Write down or discuss any thoughts or questions you may have about this, then, pray about it and submit yourself to God. Ask Him to guide you in a possible new area of your walk with Him.

----

4. In the Old Testament, Moses prayed to God for Him to appoint a new leader to be a shepherd for the congregation of the Lord. The New Testament assumes that a believer shall be a member of a congregation and that someone will care for their soul. Why could this be important? In your opinion, what does it involve to be part of a congregation? How does it relate to the leadership of a congregation?

----

5. According to Derek Prince, matters in the Church should not be settled by votes. It is God who makes the appointments. Jesus said to His apostles, "You have not chosen me, I have chosen you."

This is true of every valid function, ministry and appointment in the Church. Take some time to pray for the leadership in your church and thank God for appointing them. Pray for the Lord to appoint the right people to step up to their calling.

----

6. Read Acts 8:14-19. It is possible to be saved without having received the Holy Spirit. Why should we not be content with that? How would you respond if you met a believer who had not received the Holy Spirit?

----

7. How might the laying on of hands be used in your church to impart spiritual gifts and develop new ministry?

....

....

8. Write down or share your testimonies or examples of supernatural guidance or direction given to you by the Holy Spirit in your personal life or church.

....

....

....

....

SUMMARY

The New Testament indicates that there are numerous purposes for laying hands on other people. Unless we use this ordinance within the Church, we are missing an integral part of God's provision:

- To impart healing to the sick – to those who are unsaved/unbelievers (Mark 16:17-18; Luke 4:40-41)

- To those who are believers (James 5:14-15)

- To impart the gift of the Holy Spirit – examples of this are of the Samaritans (Acts 8:14-20); Saul of Tarsus (Acts 9:17-18); and the disciples in Ephesus. (Acts 19:1-6)

- To commission church servants (deacons) – remember that all of them had to be full of the Holy Spirit. (Acts 6:1-7)

(More purposes for laying on of hands can be found in the summary of part 3).

It is much easier to
lay hands on than to
lay hands off.

Purposes Indicated in the New Testament
(continued)

To appoint elders

The next use of laying on of hands in the New Testament is to appoint elders. In the same chapter of Acts that we have been looking at, we read:

> *They* [the two apostles, Barnabas and Paul] . . . *appointed elders in every church* . . .
> Acts 14:23

The appointment of elders initially was from the apostles.

Writing to Timothy, who was his representative in the city of Ephesus, Paul is instructing Timothy about the kind of person who should be an elder.

> *Let the elders who rule well be counted worthy of double honor, especially those who labor in the word and doctrine* [teaching].
> 1 Timothy 5:17

If you analyze the phrase "double honor," in the New Testament, it means some kind of financial remuneration. The word honor is not just an empty title, it means you show respect by the way you handle people's needs. Here we have laid out for us a standard of remuneration; those who give their time fully to the Word of God have to be remunerated by the people whom they serve, according to the amount of time they give.

Paul goes on about how to treat elders, "Do not receive an accusation against an elder except from two or three witnesses" (verse 19). That is very important. We should not entertain an accusation against a man who is in the position of an elder unless it is supported by at least two witnesses. Many times men of God have been slandered and people have taken up the slander without ever demanding witnesses. Never do that, because one of Satan's main ways of attacking people in the ministry is to raise false charges against them. Here is the protection: do not entertain an accusation against an elder unless it is supported by at least two and preferably three eyewitnesses. A great many things in the Church would change if we stuck to that rule.

Paul goes on in the same chapter:

> *I charge you before God and the Lord Jesus Christ and the elect angels that you observe these things without prejudice, doing nothing with partiality* [which has no place in the kingdom of God]. *Do not lay hands on anyone hastily* [or suddenly] *nor share in other people's sins; keep yourself pure. verses 21–22*

This is in the context of appointing elders, so when Paul says, "Do not lay hands on anyone hastily," it means we should not hastily appoint an elder. We must be very careful that we have God's mind and that the man has the qualifications required. It is much easier to lay hands on than to lay hands off. Once we have appointed an elder it is an awful problem if we have made the wrong appointment. Paul is telling Timothy to be very careful and not lay hands to appoint eldership of anybody until he is absolutely sure that it is God's choice.

Then Paul says, "Nor share in other men's sins," because if we appoint an elder who is not worthy—who may exploit the congregation and the people of God—we have a share in his sins. We must be very careful.

We see how many lessons come out of all this about laying on of hands, it is not just a little thing. The purpose of laying on of hands in all these cases—whether servants or apostles or elders—is to transmit authority, to set apart, to endorse and to equip a person for service.

To impart a spiritual gift (charisma)

Paul wrote to the Roman Christians and he said, "I would love to come to you and impart some spiritual gift to you." (See Romans 1:11.) But he didn't go at that time, he went later on. In that same context, in writing to Timothy, Paul says:

> I remind you to stir up the gift of God which is in you through the laying on of my hands.
> 2 Timothy 1:6

A gift was transmitted to Timothy through the laying on of Paul's hands. The Greek word used there is charisma, from which we get the word "charismatic." My personal opinion is that the charisma that was imparted to Timothy was apostleship. I will show you out of the Bible.

The first letter to the Thessalonians was written by three men—which was quite normal in the New Testament: Paul, Silvanus (which is another way of saying Silas) and Timothy. They were the writers of the letter. In chapter 2 of that letter, these same men—Paul, Silas and Timothy—said:

> Nor did we seek glory from men, either from you or from others, when we might have made demands as apostles of Christ.
> 1 Thessalonians 2:6

So all those three men—Paul, Silas and Timothy—were apostles. The ministry of apostles has not gone out of date because in Ephesians

4 God says He has put apostles in the church "till we all come to the unity of the faith" (verse 13). Anybody with a candid mind would have to acknowledge we have not yet come to the unity of the faith. Is that right? So, apostles, prophets, evangelists, pastors and teachers are all needed until the job is complete.

We now have four men who are called apostles besides the original Twelve: Paul, Barnabas, Silas and Timothy. They were all appointed after the Day of Pentecost. And there are many others—28 in all. (For a full explanation, see *Rediscovering God's Church* by Derek Prince Ministries–International.)

Apostleship of Timothy

I have pointed out that Timothy is called an apostle. But how did he become an apostle? This is a very important question, since we need apostles desperately in the church. Mind you, in the book of Revelation, I must point out that Jesus commended the church of Ephesus because they tested those who said they were apostles and were not, and found them to be liars (see Revelation 2:2). We should not accept everybody's claim to be an apostle — they have to be tested. We know that liars end up in the lake of fire (Revelation 21:8). This is a very serious issue. If somebody claims to be an apostle and is not, he is headed for the lake of fire.

Let's look at this situation in Acts 16. Paul has started out on his second missionary journey with Silas:

> *He came to Derbe and Lystra. And behold, a certain disciple was there, named Timothy, the son of a certain Jewish woman who believed, but his father was Greek. He was well spoken of by the brethren who were at Lystra and Iconium.*
> *Acts 16:1–2*

One thing that normally is required for anybody who is going to hold a significant position in the church is that they have a good report from their own congregation. If their own people cannot say well of them, then what other people say about them matters very little.

Years ago, a lady was sent to us from Sweden as a coworker when we were in Jerusalem. My first wife Lydia, who was very sharp, read through all the recommendations, which were many. She said, "There's just one thing missing—there's no recommendation from her own church." We took her on, but regretted it bitterly as she was a source of many problems. When choosing a person, the most important recommendation is from the people that lived with them, worked with them, and knew them. If those people do not recommend them, no other recommendation is worth much.

Timothy had a good report from the elders of the churches in which he had been ministering or living. So Paul took him along and said, "You come with me." We have to follow this rather carefully, but later on we read that Paul said to Timothy:

> Do not neglect [forget] the gift that is in you, which was given to you by prophecy with the laying on of the hands of the eldership.
> 1 Timothy 4:14

My conclusion is that a prophetic word was given saying that Timothy was to go out with Paul and Silas. On the basis of that prophetic word and because of their knowledge of his character, the local elders laid hands on Timothy and sent him out. He received the gift (or charisma) of apostleship. That is the way I understand it.

We must balance that with what we already read in 2 Timothy 1:6 where Paul says to Timothy, "Therefore I remind you to stir up the gift of God which is in you through the laying on of my hands." There could be many ways of understanding that. The most probable way is, in this situation in Lystra when the prophecy was given and duly tested (the prophecy that said Timothy was to go out with Paul and Silas), the elders said, "We endorse him." Paul said, "I receive him." Then Paul and the elders laid hands on him and imparted to him the charisma of apostleship.

It is very important to notice that the prophecy was very significant. Paul, writing to Timothy, says:

> *This charge I commit to you, son Timothy, according to the prophecies previously made concerning you, that by them you may wage the good warfare.*
> *1 Timothy 1:18*

That is the real purpose of prophecy: to encourage a person who is going to face opposition and that they will know that God has really chosen them. A quite well-known Christian leader in New Zealand had a prophecy over him when he was in the United States that revealed he was to do a certain task. He got very discouraged and he was about to give up. Then he read this verse in Timothy and he said, "I'm going to go by the prophecies." It turned out to be one of the things that got him into his ministry, which has now affected New Zealand and many other nations.

Prophecy can be very significant if given in the Holy Spirit. Much of prophecy today is what I call "Charismatic fortune-telling." People come in, lay hands on you and say, "You will do this and you will do that." Maybe— But in most cases, it just does not happen. There is a very thin line between prophecy and fortune-telling. We know that fortune-tellers can tell the truth. In Acts 16 there was a fortune-telling woman who first recognized who Paul and Silas were. Before anybody else in the city of Philippi, she knew they were "the servants of the Most High God, who proclaim to us the way of salvation." And yet, she was a servant of Satan. (See Acts 16:16–19.)

Dangers and Safeguards

Let's look at the two dangers that are mentioned. First of all, endorsing someone who is unworthy—because when we do that and it does not work out, we are partly responsible for the mess they make.

The second is what I call spiritual contamination. We may lay hands on somebody to pray for deliverance from an evil spirit, but we have to know how to protect ourselves. It can be a two-way transaction. Either we can impart the Spirit of God, or that evil spirit can affect us. I remember one occasion when I was still in the army. A group of us laid hands on a man who was suffering from severe depression. We did not really have the leading of the Lord; we just did it. Do you know what happened? We all got attacked by depression because we had not protected ourselves.

When we lay hands on somebody, we need protection. We get this by prayer and humility. We must be directed by the Holy Spirit: "As many as are led by the Spirit of God, these are the sons of God" (Romans 8:14). We must be protected by the blood of Jesus and know how to keep ourselves under the blood of Jesus.

Bear in mind that Jesus said to His disciples, "I give you authority ... over all the power of the enemy, and nothing shall by any means hurt you" (Luke 10:19).

Study Questions

Group study / personal reflection

1. What benefits could workers who are being sent out from a local church expect to receive from having hands laid on them by the elders as they are sent out?

    ----

2. According to Derek Prince, churches can be so focussed on the internal that they have little time for the real job, which is preaching the gospel to those who have never heard it. Would you agree that sharing the gospel is the most important task for any church? How does it apply to individual Christians? Prayerfully consider your role in Jesus' Great Commandment (Matthew 28:19), both privately and within your church.

---

3. Imagine a situation in your own life where you might have occasion to minister to another person through the laying on of hands. It could be for healing, ministry of the baptism in the Holy Spirit, or one of the other valid occasions for laying on of hands. How would you explain to that person why you are laying hands on them rather than "just praying for him"? See also Genesis 48:14, Numbers 27:18-23, 2 Kings 13:15-17, Mark 16:17-18, Acts 8:18, Acts 13:1-4 and Acts 6:1-6.

---

4. The Holy Spirit spoke to the church at Antioch through a prophetic word. Does the Holy Spirit still speak to the Church today, and if so, how?

---

5. Reflect/discuss: "Jesus is not here for our benefit; we are here for His glory." Write down any thoughts, objections or questions this raises with you. Prayerfully consider if there are areas where you need to repent and where your thinking needs to be aligned with God.

----

6. In 1 Timothy 5:17-19, Paul suggests two ways to treat elders. Which are they? How do you honor your elders/pastors?

Continuing with 1 Timothy 5, read verses 20-22. The Bible warns not to lay hands on an unworthy person. What safeguards can be put in place?

----

7. Read Acts 6:2-5, Acts 13:1-3 and Acts 14:23. Is prayer and fasting necessary in order to appoint leaders?

    ----

8. You have now come to the end of your study of the laying on of hands. How has your attitude or understanding regarding this foundational doctrine changed or been impacted?

    ----

9. It is essential to ensure you are protected, but as you are directed by the Holy Spirit, the laying on of hands is a God-given means to impart tremendous blessing and to establish continuity within the body of Christ. Despite this subject being taught infrequently in the church, it is a key foundational doctrine without which we will be unable to operate effectively. Ask the Lord to help you to use the laying on of hands wisely:

PRAYER

Father in heaven, I want to thank you for revealing this new truth to me. I am beginning to see the significance of laying on of hands as a means of continuity within the Church through the appointment of deacons and elders along with the commissioning of apostles. Additionally, I have come to recognize it as a means to transmitting Your power through prayer for healing, the impartation of Your Holy Spirit and His gifts.

Please help me to grow into a mature son as I am led by the Holy Spirit, and to listen for the opportunities that You give me to use this wonderful tool to Your glory. I choose to stay under the protective blood of Jesus and I thank You that as I remain prayerful and humble, that You have given me authority over all the power of the enemy and that nothing shall by any means hurt me.

In Jesus' Name, Amen

SUMMARY

There are numerous purposes for laying hands on other people:

1. To send out apostles – after fasting and prayer the church leaders in Antioch sent out their top two men. (see Acts 13:1-4)
2. To appoint elders (see Acts 6:6 and Acts 14:23). The appointment of elders initially was from the apostles.
3. To impart a spiritual gift (see 2 Timothy 1:6). The Greek word for **gift** is **charisma**.
4. Paul writes that we should not "share in other people's sins", because if we appoint a man as an elder who is not worthy, he may exploit the congregation and the people of God. If he does so, we have a share in his sins.
5. We need to protect ourselves from spiritual contamination. You may lay hands on somebody to pray for deliverance from an evil spirit but you have to know how to protect yourself because it can be a two-way transaction. Either you can impart the Spirit of God or that evil spirit can affect you.

In the next study, *At The End of Time*, Derek Prince reveals the nature of eternity and outlines what lies ahead in the realm of end-time events.

*Recall and write down the verses you memorized
at the beginning of this book:*

James 5:14

----

1 Timothy 5:22

About the Author

Derek Prince (1915–2003) was born in India of British parents. He was educated as a scholar of Greek and Latin at Eton College and King's College, Cambridge in England. Upon graduation he held a fellowship (equivalent to a professorship) in Ancient and Modern Philosophy at King's College. Prince also studied Hebrew, Aramaic, and modern languages at Cambridge and the Hebrew University in Jerusalem. As a student, he was a philosopher and self-proclaimed agnostic.

Bible Teacher

While in the British Medical Corps during World War II, Prince began to study the Bible as a philosophical work. Converted through a powerful encounter with Jesus Christ, he was baptized in the Holy Spirit a few days later. Out of this encounter, he formed two conclusions: first, that Jesus Christ is alive; second, that the Bible is a true, relevant, up-to-date book. These conclusions altered the whole course of his life, which he then devoted to studying and teaching the Bible as the Word of God.

Discharged from the army in Jerusalem in 1945, he married Lydia Christensen, founder of a children's home there. Upon their marriage, he immediately became father to Lydia's eight adopted daughters – six Jewish, one Palestinian Arab, and one English. Together, the family saw the rebirth of the state of Israel in 1948. In the late 1950s, they adopted another daughter while Prince was serving as principal of a teacher training college in Kenya.

In 1963, the Princes immigrated to the United States and pastored a church in Seattle. In 1973, Prince became one of the founders of Intercessors for America. His book Shaping History through Prayer and

Fasting has awakened Christians around the world to their responsibility to pray for their governments. Many consider underground translations of the book as instrumental in the fall of communist regimes in the USSR, East Germany, and Czechoslovakia.

Lydia Prince died in 1975, and Prince married Ruth Baker (a single mother to three adopted children) in 1978. He met his second wife, like his first wife, while she was serving the Lord in Jerusalem. Ruth died in December 1998 in Jerusalem, where they had lived since 1981.

Teaching, Preaching and Broadcasting

Until a few years before his own death in 2003 at the age of eighty-eight, Prince persisted in the ministry God had called him to as he traveled the world, imparting God's revealed truth, praying for the sick and afflicted, and sharing his prophetic insights into world events in the light of Scripture. Internationally recognized as a Bible scholar and spiritual patriarch, Derek Prince established a teaching ministry that spanned six continents and more than sixty years.

He is the author of more than fifty books, six hundred audio teachings, and one hundred video teachings, many of which have been translated and published in more than one hundred languages.

He pioneered teaching on such groundbreaking themes as generational curses, the biblical significance of Israel, and demonology. Prince's radio program, which began in 1979, has been translated into more than a dozen languages and continues to touch lives. Derek's main gift of explaining the Bible and its teaching in a clear and simple way has helped build a foundation of faith in millions of lives. His nondenominational, nonsectarian approach has made his teaching equally relevant and helpful to people from all racial and religious backgrounds, and his teaching is estimated to have reached more than half the globe.

DPM Worldwide Ministry

In 2002, he said, "It is my desire – and I believe the Lord's desire – that this ministry continue the work, which God began through me over sixty years ago, until Jesus returns." Derek Prince Ministries International continues to reach out to believers in over 140 countries with Derek's teaching, fulfilling the mandate to keep on "until Jesus returns." This is accomplished through the outreaches of more than thirty Derek Prince offices around the world, including primary work in Australia, Canada, China, France, Germany, the Netherlands, New Zealand, Norway, Russia, South Africa, Switzerland, the United Kingdom, and the United States.

For current information about these and other worldwide locations, visit **www.derekprince.com.**

FOUNDATIONS
faith life essentials

www.dpmuk.org/shop

This book is part of a series of 10 studies on the foundations of the Christian faith.

Order the other books to get everything you need to develop a strong, balanced, Spirit-filled life!

1. Founded on the Rock

There is only one foundation strong enough for the Christian life, and we must be sure our lives are built on Jesus Himself.

2. Authority and Power of God's Word

Both the Bible and Jesus Christ are identified as the Word of God. Learn how Jesus endorsed the authority of Scripture and how to use God's Word as a two-edged sword yourself.

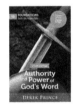

3. Through Repentance to Faith

What is faith? And how can you develop it? It starts with repentance: to change the way we think and to begin acting accordingly.

4. Faith and Works

Many Christians live in a kind of twilight - halfway between law and grace. They do not know which is which nor how to avail themselves of God's grace.

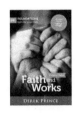

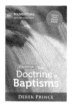

5. The Doctrine of Baptisms

A baptism is a transition - out of an old way of living into a totally new way of living. All of our being is involved. This study explains the baptism of John and the Christian (water) baptism. The baptism in the Holy Spirit is explained in 'Immersion in the Spirit'.

6. Immersion in the Spirit

Immersion can be accomplished in two ways: the swimming pool way and the Niagara Falls way. This book takes a closer look at the Niagara Falls experience, which relates to the baptism of the Holy Spirit.

7. Transmitting God's Power

Laying on of hands is one of the basic tenets of the Christian faith. By it, we may transmit God's blessing and authority and commission someone for service. Discover this Biblical doctrine!

8. At The End of Time

In this study, Derek Prince reveals the nature of eternity and outlines what lies ahead in the realm of end-time events.

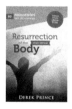

9. Resurrection of the Body

The death and resurrection of Jesus produced a change in the universe. Derek explains here how the resurrection of Jesus impacted man's spirit, soul, and body.

10. Final Judgment

This book examines the four major, successive scenes of judgment in eternity. Exploring the distinctive aspects of these four judgments, Derek opens the Scriptures to bring forth treasures hidden there.

Christian Foundations Course

If you have enjoyed this study and would like to deepen your knowledge of God's Word and apply the teaching – why not enrol on Derek Prince's Christian Foundations Bible Course?

Building on the Foundations of God's Word

A detailed study of the six essential doctrines of Christianity found in Hebrews 6:1-2.

· Scripture-based curriculum
· Practical, personal application
· Systematic Scripture memorisation
· Opportunity for questions and personal feedback from course tutor
· Certificate upon completion
· Modular based syllabus
· Set your own pace
· Affordable
· Based on *Foundational Truths for Christian Living.*

For a prospectus, application form and pricing information, please visit www.dpmuk.org, call 01462 492100 or send an e-mail to enquiries@dpmuk.org

Foundational Truths For Christian Living

Develop a strong, balanced, Spirit-filled life, by discovering the foundations of faith: salvation; baptism, the Holy Spirit, laying on hands, the believers' resurrection and eternal judgment.

Its reader-friendly format includes a comprehensive index of topics and a complete index of Scripture verses used in the book.

ISBN 978-1-908594-82-2
Paperback and eBook
£ 13.99

www.dpmuk.org/shop

More best-sellers by Derek Prince

- Blessing or Curse: You can Choose
- Bought with Blood
- Life-Changing Spiritual Power
- Marriage Covenant
- Prayers & Proclamations
- Self-Study Bible Course
- Shaping History Through Prayer and Fasting
- Spiritual Warfare for the End Times
- They Shall Expel Demons
- Who is the Holy Spirit?

For more titles: www.dpmuk.org/shop

Inspired by Derek's teaching?

Help make it available to others!

If you have been inspired and blessed by this Derek Prince resource you can help make it available to a spiritually hungry believer in other countries, such as China, the Middle East, India, Africa or Russia.

Even a small gift from you will ensure that that a pastor, Bible college student or a believer elsewhere in the world receives a free copy of a Derek Prince resource in their own language.

**Donate now: www.dpmuk.org/give
or visit www.derekprince.com**

Derek Prince Ministries

DPM–Asia/Pacific
38 Hawdon Street
Sydenham
Christchurch 8023
New Zealand
T: + 64 3 366 4443
E: admin@dpm.co.nz
W: www.dpm.co.nz

DPM–Australia
15 Park Road
Seven Hills
New South Wales 2147
Australia
T: +61 2 9838 7778
E: enquiries@au.derekprince.
com
W: www.derekprince.com.au

DPM–Canada
P. O. Box 8354
Halifax
Nova Scotia B3K 5M1
Canada
T: + 1 902 443 9577
E: enquiries.dpm@eastlink.ca
W: www.derekprince.org

DPM–France
B.P. 31, Route d'Oupia
34210 Olonzac
France
T: + 33 468 913872
E: info@derekprince.fr
W: www.derekprince.fr

DPM–Germany
Söldenhofstr. 10
83308 Trostberg
Germany
T: + 49 8621 64146
E: ibl@ibl-dpm.net
W: www.ibl-dpm.net

DPM-Netherlands
Nijverheidsweg 12
7005 BJ, Doetinchem
Netherlands
T: +31 251-255044
E: info@derekprince.nl
W: www.derekprince.nl

Offices Worldwide

DPM–Norway
P. O. Box 129
Lodderfjord
N-5881 Bergen
Norway
T: +47 928 39855
E: xpress@dpskandinavia.com
W: www.derekprince.no

Derek Prince Publications Pte. Ltd.
P. O. Box 2046
Robinson Road Post Office
Singapore 904046
T: + 65 6392 1812
E: dpmchina@singnet.com.sg
W: www.dpmchina.org (English)
    www.ygmweb.org (Chinese)

DPM–South Africa
P. O. Box 33367
Glenstantia
0010 Pretoria
South Africa
T: +27 12 348 9537
E: enquiries@derekprince.co.za
W: www.derekprince.co.za

DPM–Switzerland
Alpenblick 8
CH-8934 Knonau
Switzerland
T: + 41 44 768 25 06
E: dpm-ch@ibl-dpm.net
W: www.ibl-dpm.net

DPM–UK
PO Box 393
Hitchin SG5 9EU
United Kingdom
T: + 44 1462 492100
E: enquiries@dpmuk.org
W: www.dpmuk.org

DPM–USA
P. O. Box 19501
Charlotte NC 28219
USA
T: + 1 704 357 3556
E: ContactUs@derekprince.org
W: www.derekprince.org